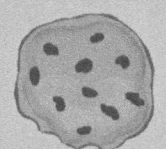
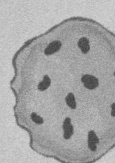
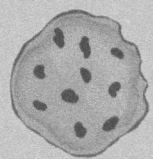
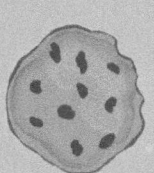
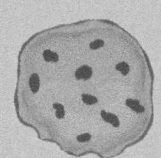
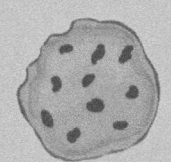

By Brenda Finger

Illustrated by Anna Wochnick

Scout the Sloth Book Series!

Scout the Sloth is cute, cuddly, and full of adventure. Scout's Adventure Map brings his adventures to life by illustrating the journey through the book series. Follow his footprints on the unique and fun adventure that we call Scout the Sloth Book Series! Scout begins every journey with his hat and backpack so grab yours and step into the map for the adventure of a lifetime! Now turn the page and let the Scout adventures begin!

Scout BOOKS

All About Scout the Sloth
Scout Sliding into School
Scout Getting Messy at the Bakery
Scout Decorating for Christmas
Scout Exploring the Zoo
Scout Digging at the Construction Site
Scout Harvesting at the Farm
Scout Driving into the Auto Shop
Scout Brushing at the Dentist
Scout Making Friends at the Pet Shop
Scout Relaxing on Vacation
Scout Planting at the Garden Center
Scout Investigating at the Fire Station
Scout Playing at the Fair
Scout Hiking around the Campsite
Scout Performing at the Theatre
Scout Sorting at the Post Office
Scout Blasting off in the Space Station

Explore www.scoutthesloth.com

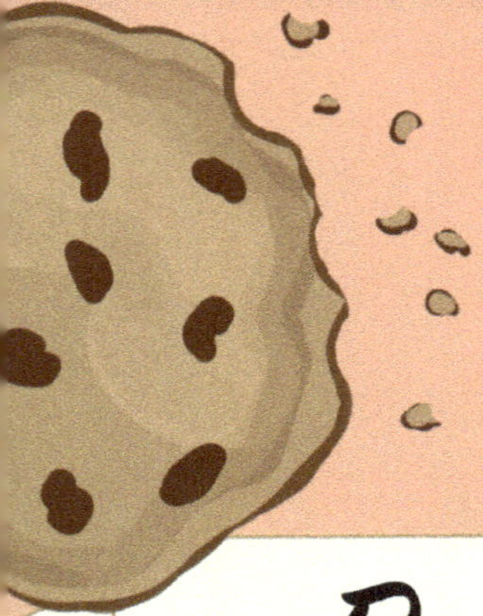

Recipe

Scout the Sloth book series are great tools for early and elementary teachers along with homeschooling programs.

Visit our website at www.scoutthesloth.com

Copyright © by Brenda Finger and Anna Wochnick

All rights reserved. No part of this publication may be produced in any form or by any electronic or mechanical means, including information storage and retrieval systems, without permission in writing by the author and illustrator. For information regarding permission, contact the author and/or illustrator at abscoutseries@gmail.com

Printed in U.S.A.

ISBN-9780578328591

The artist used Adobe Photoshop and Adobe Illustrator to create the illustrations for this book.

By Brenda Finger

Illustrated by Anna Wochnick

I hop on the bus to take our first field trip.

We are going to get messy at the bakery.

The bake shop is down the street.

I can already taste the goodies on my lip.

The bus stops at the front door.

I look up with stary eyes.

To pictures of cakes, cookies, and pies.

We walk into the front door.

I can smell all the sweet treats.

I want to eat everything and more.

Bakers make desserts look so yummy.

Bright colors of frosting and icing

make a rumble in my tummy.

The kitchen is full of baking tools from

pots, pans, and cookie sheets.

To stoves, ovens, cups, and plates.

This place is full of treats.

A cup of this.

A dash of that.

A sugar sprinkle

can make the cakes fat.

We are making a cupcake.

I measure sugar and flour then crack an egg.

They will have sprinkle frosting.

The children will start to beg.

I can smell the sweet smells of cupcakes and pies.

I hear the jingle of the doorbell outside.

The doorbell tells us there are customers coming to buy.

I just know they are going to want the cupcake and pies.

We are done with our work.

It is time to pick the treats.

The baker has prepared a platter full.

We can each have two.

Oh! What will I pick to taste and chew?

I chose a cookie and a chocolate cake pop.

I had to snitch a taste but got all messy.

I put my treats in a bag and had to stop.

It was so much fun at the bakery shop.

The bakery fun has come to an end.

We look and see the construction site.

Will it be a chance to drive, dig, or pretend?

Get to know us..

Brenda Finger is an author and educator. She earned her undergraduate degree from Minnesota State University Moorhead with emphasis in early, elementary, and special education. She then continued and received her doctorate in management from Colorado Technical University in Colorado Springs Colorado. She and her husband own a childcare center where she teaches the pre-kindergarten children. She enjoys gardening and spending time with her grandchildren.

Anna Wochnick is an illustrator and painter. She is from Cold Spring Minnesota and earned her Bachelor of Science degree with an emphasis in graphic design and minor in psychology at North Dakota State University. She enjoys running and biking. She spends time outdoors and relaxing at the lake with family and friends.

Our story began in Fargo, North Dakota in 2018, where we started teaching pre-kindergarten children together. Little did we know this was just the beginning for us! Not only do we enjoy teaching as a team, but we developed a friendship along the way. One day we decided we wanted to do more for children and impact their knowledge in another way. This is where Scout the Sloth book series began. We combined our passion for teaching pre-kindergarten children and our loving partnership to write and illustrate children's books. Every book is an adventure for Scout, the children, and for us. We would love for you to be a part of our adventure.

www.ingramcontent.com/pod-product-compliance
Lightning Source LLC
Chambersburg PA
CBHW061801290426
44109CB00030B/2920